MYSTERIES OF THE HOME

Paula Meehan was born and lives in Dublin. She has published four books of poetry, her major work appearing in two collections from her Irish publisher, the Gallery Press, *The Man who was Marked by Winter* (1991) and *Pillow Talk* (1994), both shortlisted for the prestigious *Irish Times*/Aer Lingus Irish Literature Prize. *Mysteries of the Home*, a selection drawing on those two books, was published by Bloodaxe in 1996. Her poems have been selected for numerous anthologies, including *Sixty Women Poets, The New Poetry* and *Dublines* from Bloodaxe.

She writes for the theatre, for TEAM, Ireland's premier theatre-in-education company, and has collaborated with contemporary dance companies, musicians and visual artists. As well as holding creative writing fellowships at Trinity College and University College Dublin, she has worked with several inner city communities, especially in the area of Dublin north of the Liffey where she grew up, and for the last ten years has run workshops in various prisons, most frequently with women prisoners in Mountjoy. She has received two Bursaries in Literature from the Irish Arts Council and in 1995 received the Martin Toonder Award for Literature.

PAULA MEEHAN

✸

Mysteries
of the Home

BLOODAXE BOOKS

ISBN: 1 85224 374 0

First published 1996 by
Bloodaxe Books Ltd,
P.O. Box 1SN,
Newcastle upon Tyne NE99 1SN.

Bloodaxe Books Ltd acknowledges
the financial assistance of Northern Arts.

Cover printing by J. Thomson Colour Printers Ltd, Glasgow.

Printed in Great Britain by
Cromwell Press Ltd, Broughton Gifford, Melksham, Wiltshire.

in memory of my mother
HELENA
1933–1975

Acknowledgements

Mysteries of the Home is a selection from two collections published in Ireland by the Gallery Press: *The Man who was Marked by Winter* (1991) and *Pillow Talk* (1994), the former including poems first published by Beaver Row Press in *Return and No Blame* (1984) and *Reading the Sky* (1986).

Contents

Well

I know this path by magic not by sight.
Behind me on the hillside the cottage light
is like a star that's gone astray. The moon
is waning fast, each blade of grass a rune
inscribed by hoarfrost. This path's well worn.
I lug a bucket by bramble and blossoming blackthorn.
I know this path by magic not by sight.
Next morning when I come home quite unkempt
I cannot tell what happened at the well.
You spurn my explanation of a sex spell
cast by the spirit who guards the source
that boils deep in the belly of the earth,
even when I show you what lies strewn
in my bucket – a golden waning moon,
seven silver stars, our own porch light,
your face at the window staring into the dark.

The Pattern

Little has come down to me of hers,
a sewing machine, a wedding band,
a clutch of photos, the sting of her hand
across my face in one of our wars

when we had grown bitter and apart.
Some say that's the fate of the eldest daughter.
I wish now she'd lasted till after
I'd grown up. We might have made a new start

as women without tags like *mother, wife,*
sister, daughter, taken our chances from there.
At forty-two she headed for god knows where.
I've never gone back to visit her grave.

*

First she'd scrub the floor with Sunlight soap,
an armreach at a time. When her knees grew sore
she'd break for a cup of tea, then start again
at the door with lavender polish. The smell
would percolate back through the flat to us,
her brood banished to the bedroom.

And as she buffed the wax to a high shine
did she catch her own face coming clear?
Did she net a glimmer of her true self?
Did her mirror tell what mine tells me?

I have her shrug and go on
knowing history has brought her to her knees.

She'd call us in and let us skate around
in our socks. We'd grow solemn as planets
in an intricate orbit about her.

*

She's bending over crimson cloth,
the younger kids are long in bed.
Late summer, cold enough for a fire,
she works by fading light
to remake an old dress for me.
It's first day back at school tomorrow.

*

'Pure lambswool. Plenty of wear in it yet.
You know I wore this when I went out with your Da.
I was supposed to be down in a friend's house,
your Granda caught us at the corner.
He dragged me in by the hair – it was long as yours then –
in front of the whole street.
He called your Da every name under the sun,
cornerboy, lout; I needn't tell you
what he called me. He shoved my whole head
under the kitchen tap, took a scrubbing brush
and carbolic soap and in ice-cold water he scrubbed
every spick of lipstick and mascara off my face.
Christ but he was a right tyrant, your Granda.
It'll be over my dead body anyone harms a hair of your head.'

*

She must have stayed up half the night
to finish the dress. I found it airing at the fire,
three new copybooks on the table and a bright
bronze nib, St Christopher strung on a silver wire,

as if I were embarking on a perilous journey
to uncharted realms. I wore that dress
with little grace. To me it spelt poverty,
the stigma of the second hand. I grew enough to pass

it on by Christmas to the next in line. I was sizing
up the world beyond our flat patch by patch
daily after school, and fitting each surprising
city street to city square to diamond. I'd watch

the Liffey for hours pulsing to the sea
and the coming and going of ships,
certain that one day it would carry me
to Zanzibar, Bombay, the Land of the Ethiops.

*

There's a photo of her taken in the Phoenix Park
alone on a bench surrounded by roses
as if she had been born to formal gardens.
She stares out as if unaware
that any human hand held the camera, wrapped
entirely in her own shadow, the world beyond her
already a dream, already lost. She's
eight months pregnant. Her last child.

*

Her steel needles sparked and clacked,
the only other sound a settling coal
or her sporadic mutter
at a hard part in the pattern.
She favoured sensible shades:
Moss Green, Mustard, Beige.

I dreamt a robe of a colour
so pure it became a word.

Sometimes I'd have to kneel
an hour before her by the fire,
a skein around my outstretched hands,
while she rolled wool into balls.
If I swam like a kite too high
amongst the shadows on the ceiling
or flew like a fish in the pools
of pulsing light, she'd reel me firmly
home, she'd land me at her knees.

Tongues of flame in her dark eyes,
she'd say, 'One of these days I must
teach you to follow a pattern.'

Ard Fheis

Down through the cigarette smoke
the high windows cast
ecstatic light to the floorboards
stiletto pocked and butt scorched

but now such golden pools of sun to bask in there.
I am fish
water my demesne.
The room pulses in, then out, of focus

and all this talk of the people, of who we are,
of what we need, is robbed of meaning,
becomes sub-melody, sonic undertow,
a room of children chanting off

by heart a verse. I'm nine or ten,
the Central Model School,
Miss Shannon beats out the metre
with her stick.

I wind up in the ghost place
the language rocks me to,
a cobwebby state, chilled vault
littered with our totems;

a tattered Starry Plough,
a bloodstained Proclamation,
Connolly strapped wounded to a chair,
May blossom in Kilmainham.

I am following my father's steps
on a rainy Sunday in the National Museum,
by talisman of torc, carved spiral,
síle na gig's yoni made luscious in stone.

And somewhere there is vestige
of my mother nursing me to sleep,
when all my world was touch,
and possibly was peace.

I float down to a September evening,
the Pro-Cathedral, girls in rows at prayer,
gaze at the monstrance, lulled to adoration,
mesmeric in frankincense and candlelight:

Hail our life our sweetness and our hope
to thee do we cry poor banished children of Eve
to thee do we send up our sighs
mourning and weeping in this valley of tears.

I push back to the surface, break clear,
the light has come on fluorescent
and banishes my dreaming self.
It is, after all, an ordinary room

and we are ordinary people.
We pull our collars up and head
for the new moon sky of our city
fondling each whorled bead in our macabre rosary.

Don't even speak to me of Stephen the Martyr,
the host snug in his palm,
slipping through the wounded streets
to keep his secret safe.

Buying Winkles

My mother would spare me sixpence and say,
'Hurry up now and don't be talking to strange
men on the way.' I'd dash from the ghosts
on the stairs where the bulb had blown
out into Gardiner Street, all relief.
A bonus if the moon was in the strip of sky
between the tall houses, or stars out,
but even in rain I was happy – the winkles
would be wet and glisten blue like little
night skies themselves. I'd hold the tanner tight
and jump every crack in the pavement,
I'd wave up to women at sills or those
lingering in doorways and weave a glad path through
men heading out for the night.

She'd be sitting outside the Rosebowl Bar
on an orange-crate, a pram loaded
with pails of winkles before her.
When the bar doors swung open they'd leak
the smell of men together with drink
and I'd see light in golden mirrors.
I envied each soul in the hot interior.

I'd ask her again to show me the right way
to do *it*. She'd take a pin from her shawl –
'Open the eyelid. So. Stick it in
till you feel a grip, then slither him out.
Gently, mind.' The sweetest extra winkle
that brought the sea to me.
'Tell yer Ma I picked them fresh this morning.'

I'd bear the newspaper twists
bulging fat with winkles
proudly home, like torches.

Child Burial

Your coffin looked unreal,
fancy as a wedding cake.

I chose your grave clothes with care,
your favourite stripey shirt,

your blue cotton trousers.
They smelt of woodsmoke, of October,

your own smell there too.
I chose a gansy of handspun wool,

warm and fleecy for you. It is
so cold down in the dark.

No light can reach you and teach you
the paths of wild birds,

the names of the flowers,
the fishes, the creatures.

Ignorant you must remain
of the sun and its work,

my lamb, my calf, my eaglet,
my cub, my kid, my nestling,

my suckling, my colt. I would spin
time back, take you again

within my womb, your amniotic lair,
and further spin you back

through nine waxing months
to the split seeding moment

you chose to be made flesh,
word within me.

I'd cancel the love feast
the hot night of your making.

I would travel alone
to a quiet mossy place,

you would spill from me into the earth
drop by bright red drop.

Her Heroin Dream

She dreamt the moon a gaudy egg,
a Chinese gimcrack. When it hatched,
a young dragon would spiral to earth
trailing garnet and emerald sparks,
shrieking through the ozone layer,
the citizens blinded by dragon-glory.

In the heart of night would blaze a light
greater than the sun, supernova fierce.

The Liffey and the two canals would vanish
and Dublin bay evaporate, leaving beached
spiny prawns and crabs, coiled sea snails,
a dead sailor's shoe, shipping wrecks,
radioactive waste in Saharas of sand.
The buildings would scorch to black stumps,
windows melt, railroads buckle,
bricks fallen to dust would sift
in dervish swirls along the thoroughfares.

Each tree in the town would turn torch
to celebrate his passing.

She would wait in her cell.
He'd enter softly in the guise of a youth:
his eyes the blue of hyacinth,
his skin like valerian,
his lips Parthian red.
He'd take her from behind.

The kundalini energy would shoot straight up her spine,
blow her head open like a flower.
Dragon seed would root deep in her womb.
Dragon nature course through her veins.

They'd slip from the cell hands twined,
glide over the prison wall into a new morning
to sport among the ruins.

The Dark Twin

You believe
they contract when you turn to the window –
there's a girl in pink passing
you might or might not know
down a street you say history will be made on
as the woman you hold turns to your eyes.
Anemones, she tells you, make the same sound as pupils.
Pishew, pishew, were you close enough
in rockpool silence, is what you'd hear.

And you believe
she'll turn again and again to your eyes
as you hold her. Show your stored wisdom
in a ritual of healing. Your hands move
over her dark form. She can't refuse you.
Gulls cross the sky, bells sound for first Mass.
You know she'll seek you for she is
your dark twin. Her eyes don't reflect you.
Her pupils are still as the dark pool
she grew from. She names you *diablo*.
If you enter her now you can teach her
the nature of history, the city that's made her.
She'll name a price later and say you've had
her cheaply. She'll be just. You won't haggle
but find the exact change and count it into her palm.

And you believe
she'll return and desire you once more –
more than her own life, more than her darkness.
This you know surely as you glance over
her eyes to the girl in pink passing.
You move above her: by your ritual rocking
you'll move her to tears.
She'll learn to accept love though still
you must pay her the exact amount due.

And you believe
you can quieten her sobs in the morning
when she tells you again
how the world will succumb to men in dark uniforms.
You believe she has stood, her face to a stone wall,
while the men cock their rifles and wait for the order.
You know she's been there. You know you can heal her.
She is your dark twin. You know you must heal her.
The burns from the bombings will ease as you rock her.
The legs that are mangled made whole for fast dancing.
Her sobs will be songs for the rearing of children.
Still you must pay her the exact amount due.

And you believe all this
as you turn from the window,
the girl in pink passing at the moment
you enter your dark twin. Your pupils
dilate, your breath as it leaves you
makes the one word you can never repay her.

Lullaby

(for Brenda Meehan)

My sister is sleeping
and makes small murmurs
as she turns in a dream

she is swinging a child
under the shade of
a lilac tree blooming

in a garden in springtime
my sister is sleeping.

The rain falls
on Finglas
to each black roof

it lashes a story
of time on the ocean
of moon on the river

and flashes down drainpipes
into deep gutters.

My sister is sleeping
her hands full of blossoms
plucked for the child

who dreams in her womb
rocked in tall branches
close to the stars

where my sister is sleeping
within her small child.

The Statue of the Virgin at Granard Speaks

It can be bitter here at times like this,
November wind sweeping across the border.
Its seeds of ice would cut you to the quick.
The whole town tucked up safe and dreaming,
even wild things gone to earth, and I
stuck up here in this grotto, without as much as
star or planet to ease my vigil.

The howling won't let up. Trees
cavort in agony as if they would be free
and take off – ghost voyagers
on the wind that carries intimations
of garrison towns, walled cities, ghetto lanes
where men hunt each other and invoke
the various names of God as blessing
on their death tactics, their night manoeuvres.
Closer to home the wind sails over
dying lakes. I hear fish drowning.
I taste the stagnant water mingled
with turf smoke from outlying farms.

They call me Mary – Blessed, Holy, Virgin.
They fit me to a myth of a man crucified:
the scourging and the falling, and the falling again,
the thorny crown, the hammer blow of iron
into wrist and ankle, the sacred bleeding heart.
They name me Mother of all this grief
though mated to no mortal man.
They kneel before me and their prayers
fly up like sparks from a bonfire
that blaze a moment, then wink out.

It can be lovely here at times. Springtime,
early summer. Girls in Communion frocks
pale rivals to the riot in the hedgerows
of cow parsley and haw blossom, the perfume
from every rushy acre that's left for hay
when the light swings longer with the sun's push north.

Or the grace of a midsummer wedding
when the earth herself calls out for coupling
and I would break loose of my stony robes,
pure blue, pure white, as if they had robbed
a child's sky for their colour. My being
cries out to be incarnate, incarnate,
maculate and tousled in a honeyed bed.

Even an autumn burial can work its own pageantry.
The hedges heavy with the burden of fruiting
crab, sloe, berry, hip; clouds scud east
pear scented, windfalls secret in long
orchard grasses, and some old soul is lowered
to his kin. Death is just another harvest
scripted to the season's play.

But on this All Souls' Night there is
no respite from the keening of the wind.
I would not be amazed if every corpse came risen
from the graveyard to join in exaltation with the gale,
a cacophony of bone imploring sky for judgement
and release from being the conscience of the town.

On a night like this I remember the child
who came with fifteen summers to her name,
and she lay down alone at my feet
without midwife or doctor or friend to hold her hand
and she pushed her secret out into the night,
far from the town tucked up in little scandals,
bargains struck, words broken, prayers, promises,
and though she cried out to me in extremis
I did not move,
I didn't lift a finger to help her,
I didn't intercede with heaven,
nor whisper the charmed word in God's ear.

On a night like this I number the days to the solstice
and the turn back to the light.
                              O sun,
centre of our foolish dance,
burning heart of stone,
molten mother of us all,
hear me and have pity.

Home by Starlight

(for Lisa Steppe)

You ask me which I prefer –
the stars themselves or their mirror
image on the puddles of our path
home. Their light as strong
as moonlight, the night cold and still.
We take a shortcut across an overgrown rath,
old stones that seem to spill
haphazardly, but if you haul back the long
ivy tendrils, hack through the brambles, you
will find patterns there, you

will know lifetimes ago we gazed
at the same constellations amazed
by such brilliance, and found in their rule
the measure of each year, each journey.
Do you remember how it was?
The seasons of study in the star school
scanning for portent conjugations
of sky beasts which peopled the sea
of our heavens. Do you remember
that crazy light we tracked one mid-winter?

The light they later called the Christos,
and the terror, the blood cost of that Logos?
How our arts were eclipsed and many
gentle comrades tortured and burned?
How the songs we had crafted for travel
were lost, language itself lost, when we
were scattered like sparks to the wind? So well
you might ask – the light, or its image, turned
in a puddle, surefooted friend on the path you roam
by the light of a million million suns home.

Two Buck Tim from Timbuctoo

I found it in the granary under rubble
where the back gable caved in,
a 78 miraculously whole in a nest of smashed records,
as if it had been hatched by a surreal hen,
a pullet with a taste for the exotic.

I took it in and swabbed it down,
put it on the turntable and filled the cottage
with its scratchy din. Ghosts of the long dead
flocked from their narrow grooves beneath foreign soils
to foxtrot round my kitchen in the dusk.

I'd say Leitrim in the forties was every bit as depressed
as Leitrim is today, the young were heading off
in droves, the same rain fell all winter long.
Eventually one old woman was left looking at her hands
while the Bell Boys of Broadway played 'Two Buck Tim from
        Timbuctoo',

and dreamt her daughters back about the place, the swing of a skirt,
a face caught in lamplight, with every revolution of the disc.
This winter I have grown unduly broody. As I go
about my daily work an otherworldly mantra turns
within my head: Two Buck Tim from Timbuctoo,

Two Buck Tim from Timbuctoo. It keeps me up at night.
I roam about the rooms. I hope to catch them at it.
I want to rend the veil, step out onto their plane,
spiral down a rain-washed road, let some ghostly partner
take the lead, become at last another migrant soul.

My Love about his Business in the Barn

You're fiddling with something in the barn,
a makeshift yoke for beans to climb,
held together like much in our lives
with blue baling twine, scraps of chicken wire.

Such a useless handyman: our world could collapse,
frequently *has* with a huff and a puff.
You'd hoke a length of string from your back pocket,
humming a Woody Guthrie song, you'd bind

the lintel to stone, the slate to rafter,
'It'll do for the minute if the wind stays down.'
And so I've learned to live with dodgy matter:
shelves that tumble to the floor if you glance

at them sideways; walls that were not built
for leaning against; a great chasm in the kitchen
crossable only by a rope bridge; a blow hole
by our bed where the Atlantic spouts.

On stormy nights it drenches the walls, the ceiling.
Days you come home reeking of *Brut* and brimstone
I suspect you've been philandering underground
and not breaking your back beyond on the bog.

So is it any wonder when I see you
mooching in the barn this fine May morning,
a charm of finches lending local colour,
that I rush for my holy water, my rabbit's foot?

That I shut my eyes tight and wait
for the explosion, then the silence,
then the sweet aftershock when the earth skids
under me, when stars and deep space usurp my day?

Zugzwang

She fills jugs of water at the sink
for flowers: mignonette, cotton lavender,
for their scent and fretty form,
sweet pea and love-lies-bleeding,
a token of domestic tragedy, a wound.

He looks up from the chessboard where
he's replaying a famous game of Capablanca's.
He catches her off guard, murmuring
to herself, framed by the door, the blooms.
She wears a dress for a change,
of a sea blue that ebbs to green
when sun floods the kitchen.
Beyond is the window. The sky is an ocean
where clouds like spacecraft or cuban cigars
float towards the mountain.
He imagines Dutch paintings, bourgeois
interiors, *Woman Washing, Woman Setting
a Table, Woman Bending over a Child*
and conjures a painting half made –
Woman Surrounded by Flowers at a Sink,
himself at an easel mixing pigment and oil,
a north facing studio above a canal
where barges are waiting their turn at the lock
and on the Zuyder Zee scuppy waves rock sailboats.
The landscape surrenders to a polar light.

She arranges the flowers in two jugs.
Lately she has heard her dead mother's voice
tumbling in the drier with the wash:
I told you so, I told you so, I told you so.
The women on the TV in their business suits
and white teeth transmit coded messages,
escape maps buried in their speeches,
though they appear to be reading the news
lest others are watching. Soldiers
have set up a barricade down the road;
they are part of a nationwide search
for a desperate man and his hostage.

A jug in each hand, she moves to the table
and he fancies she has stepped straight into
a Cretan mosaic, a priestess in a Minoan rite,
devotee of the bull, and himself a mosaic worker
fingering a thousand fragments until he finds
the exact shade of blue with that green undertow
to fit his pattern. For her face
and breasts he would use tiles of pure gold;
the alchemists hold it has the exact
calibration of human skin. He will not dwell

on last week's events when he woke
in the night and she was gone. He found her
digging in the garden, her nightgown
drenched through, muck smeared on her arms,
on her legs, the rain lashing down.
She explained that she wanted to be close
to her loved ones, her lost ones, that
they are so cold and lonely in the earth
and they long for the warmth of the living.

She places the flowers on the table.
Any day now she will let go her grip,
surrender herself to the ecstatic freefall.
We are all aware that when she hits bottom
she will shatter into smithereens.
Each shard will reflect the room, the flowers,
the chessboard, and her beloved sky beyond
like a calm ocean lapping at the mountain.

Coda

You open the hated book,
the book of my self.
The more that you read there
the fainter the print becomes
until the letters are faded,
white nests protected by the page.

I gave up on the window box:
leaves went transparent,
eaten away by greenfly.
When you come home you'll find
geranium ghosts, spectral nasturtiums,
a flock of albino butterflies
settled on the sill. I'll be hung

up in the larder by the heels,
dressed as a deer would be,
my skin in a casual heap on the floor.
You can wear it if you wish
though flesh clings to parts,
especially the extremities. Still,
a sharp flint stone could do the trick.

It should be a comfortable fit.
There's a note in the dresser
on French seams and buttonholes
lest you need to alter any part.
The breasts will be a problem;
you'll need the smallest crewel for the job
and the good new scissors of German steel.
The offcuts may be useful somewhere else.

Put the rest of me on at gas mark 3,
(you know those stringy muscles in my back!).
Don't forget to baste me now and then.

Don't bring your current lover home to tea,
there's just enough for one. Besides
I'm an acquired taste, like squid
or pickled limes. I wouldn't delay –
were I you I'd catch the earliest ferry
else the worms will have their way with me.

You'd come upon me bleached and empty
in the cool larder rafters, the slates blown down,
green garden light nesting in my bones.

The Man who was Marked by Winter

He was heading for Bridal Veil Falls,
an upward slog on a dusty path.
Mid May and hot as a mill-

stone grinding his shoulders, his back.
Each breath was a drowning.
And who's to say if it was a mirage

the other side of the creek's brown
water. He saw it, that's enough,
in the deep shade of a rocky overhang –

the spoor of winter, a tracery of ice. If
we'd reached him, we'd have warned him of the depth,
the secret current underneath.

He must have been half crazy with the heat.
He stripped off. Waded in.
His feet were cut from under him. He was swept

downriver in melt water from the mountain.
She clutched him to her breast, that beast of winter.
One look from her agate eyes and he abandoned

hope. He was pliant. She pulled him under.
If she had him once, she had him thrice.
She shook his heart and mind asunder.

And he would willingly have gone back to her palace
or her lair, whichever; whatever she was,
he would have lived forever in her realms of ice.

She must have grown tired of his human ways.
We found him tossed like a scrap on the bank,
hours or years or seconds later. His eyes

stared straight at the sun. His past is a blank
snowfield where no one will step. She made her mark
below his heart, a five-fingered gash – *Bondsman*.

Three Paintings of York Street
(for Ita Kelly)

Before the Pubs Close

Quick. Before the moon is eaten
by that cloud, rescue its dust,
sift it over the shopping centre,
the student hostel, that couple
hand in hand walking to the Green.
And quick. Before last orders and drunken cries
steal the breath the street is holding,
exhale it lovingly below each window
to reclaim from night the shadowy areas.

Salt your canvas with a woman
quietly weeping in a tenement room
until her tears become a blessing
sprinkled from your fingers,
those spatters of intense blue
beside the three black cats
who wait with…patience, is it?,
on a granite step for you to find
the exact amber of their eyes
as they gaze at the moon.

Woman Found Dead behind Salvation Army Hostel

You will have to go outside for this one.
The night is bitter cold
but you must go out,
you could not invent this.

You can make a quick sketch
and later, in your studio, mix the colours,
the purple, the eerie green of her bruises,
the garish crimson of her broken mouth.

For consolation there's the line
her spine makes as it remembers
its beginnings, as if at the very end
she turned foetal and knew again
the roar of her mother's blood in her ears,
the drum of her mother's heart
before she drowned in the seventh wave
beyond pain, or your pity.

Your hand will steady as you draw the cobbles.
They impose a discipline, the comfort of habit,
as does the symmetry of brick walls
which define the alley and whose very height
cut off the light and hid
the beast who maimed her.

Children of York Street at Play in the College of Surgeons' Carpark

You worry given the subject
about sentimentality, about indulgence,
but as you work
the children turn to pattern
and you may as well be
weaving in a Turkish bazaar, one eye
on your son lest he topple to the tarmac.
And your fingers of their own volition
find the perfect stress between warp and weft.
Your mind can lope as loosely
as a gazelle through savannah
or nimble as a mountain goat,
attain an unexpected purchase on a sheer
cliff face, or you may be dolphin
and cavort the prismatic ranges
of the green sea's depth.
                          And after,
cleaning brushes, you will wonder
why no child can be discerned
on your canvas, why there is no bike,
no skateboard, no skipping rope,
no carpark, why your colours are
all primary, pure as you can make them,
why in your pattern the shapes keep shifting
like flighty spirits threatening
to burst into song.

My Father Perceived as a Vision of St Francis

(for Brendan Kennelly)

It was the piebald horse in next door's garden
frightened me out of a dream
with her dawn whinny. I was back
in the boxroom of the house,
my brother's room now,
full of ties and sweaters and secrets.
Bottles chinked on the doorstep,
the first bus pulled up to the stop.
The rest of the house slept

except for my father. I heard
him rake the ash from the grate,
plug in the kettle, hum a snatch of a tune.
Then he unlocked the back door
and stepped out into the garden.

Autumn was nearly done, the first frost
whitened the slates of the estate.
He was older than I had reckoned,
his hair completely silver,
and for the first time I saw the stoop
of his shoulder, saw that
his leg was stiff. What's he at?
So early and still stars in the west?

They came then: birds
of every size, shape, colour; they came
from the hedges and shrubs,
from eaves and garden sheds,
from the industrial estate, outlying fields,
from Dubber Cross they came
and the ditches of the North Road.
The garden was a pandemonium
when my father threw up his hands
and tossed the crumbs to the air. The sun

cleared O'Reilly's chimney
and he was suddenly radiant,
a perfect vision of St Francis,
made whole, made young again,
in a Finglas garden.

A Child's Map of Dublin

I wanted to find you Connolly's Starry Plough,
the flag I have lived under since birth or since
I first scanned nightskies and learned the nature of work.
'That hasn't been on show in years,' the porter told us.
They're revising at the National Museum,
all hammers and drills and dust, converting to
an interpretive centre in the usual contemporary style.

The Natural History Museum: found poem
of oriole, kingfisher, sparrowhawk, nightjar,
but the gull drew me strongest – childhood guide
to the freedom and ecstasy of flight. Common
cacophonist, nothing romantic about that squabbler
of windowledges, invader of the one p.m. schoolyard,
wakefollower of sailors. But watch him on a clear ocean

and nothing reads the wind so well. In the updraught
of a sudden love, I walk the northside streets
that whelped me; not a brick remains
of the tenement I reached the age of reason in. Whole
streets are remade, the cranes erect over Eurocrat schemes
down the docks. There is nothing
to show you there, not a trace of a girl

in ankle socks and hand-me-downs, sulking
on a granite step when she can't raise the price of a film,
or a bus to the beach. The movie she ran in her head?
Africa – hostage slave to some Berber prince or, chainmailed,
she is heroine of a hopeless war
spurring her men to death, but honourable death.

Better I take you up Cumberland Street Saturday.
We'll hoke out something foreign and erotic,
from the mounds of cast-offs on the path.
And when the market's over we'll wander home,
only go the streets that are our fancy.
You'll ask me no questions. I'll tell you no lies.

Climb in here between the sheets
in the last light of this April evening. We'll trust
the charts of our bodies. They've brought us
safe to each other, battle-scarred and frayed
at the folds, they'll guide us to many wonders.
Come, let's play in the backstreets and tidal flats
till we fall off the edge of the known world,

and drown.

The Other Woman

That night when you entered her for the first time
she was the lonely city, and you were a man with a key
to a room in a house on a street where you might go out of the rain
and sit by the window to drink lemon vodka

with no tales to tell, no questions, no answers, no
hope of tomorrow. Not silence; but breath and the fall
of rain to the garden. No light but streetlight.
She was in shadow. You were a stranger and all

she could trust was what she read of your path
when you held out your hand and said come.
She was scribed on your fateline, her own name there
was a song half-remembered, hot on your tongue,

hot on the white sheets you tangled your selves up in.
They were your sails and she was the port in every girl
you knew you were born free for; and bound
to the rule of the sea, her grief, her pulse, her moody

river, her sulky moons, the way they hid for months
under cloud, you were humble. I understood all this
when she woke the next morning to rain on the city.
For my work I need starlight preferably

and plenty of time on my hands. I made her dream
sunshine, a tower, a golden fish atop it, a street
running down to a harbour, a ship just docked,
a stranger approaching with the key to her door.

Handmaid

Lord, when I walked with you under the stars
and we were overcome by desire
and we lay down in the desert night,
I fell into your eyes, tasted your salt.

And, Lord, when I was impaled on you,
gazed on your face with devotion,
you spoke of the hard day's ride
and distances you had crossed to couple with me.

I have opened wide as a rivermouth to you
and would have you invade my cells,
my womb, my heart, my head, O Lordy
do with me what you will.

City

1 *Hearth*

What is the fire you draw to
when you clutch each other
between the sheets? What cold do
you fear? What drives you near
madness, the jealousy you daily
bear? That tyrant time
sifting through the glass? Tell me
a story, not in rhyme
or made up fancy but plain
as the ash in the grate.
The windowpane rattles, the rain
beats about the house. Late
drinkers are turfed from the bar. Wind
snatches their song, tosses it down-
river to the sea pulsing in your mind.
You slip your moorings, cruise the town.

Out here you can breathe.
Between showers, the street
empty. Forget your lover
faithless in the chilly bed
who'll wake soon and wonder
if you've left for good.
Granite under your feet
glitters, nearby a siren. Threat

or a promise? You take Fumbally Lane
to the Blackpitts, cut back by the canal.
Hardly a sound you've made, creature
of night in grey jeans and desert boots,
familiar of shade. Listen.
                              The train
bearing chemicals to Mayo, a dog far off, the fall
of petals to the paths of the Square,
a child screaming in a third floor flat.

On Mount Street high heels clack,
stumble in their rhythm, resume.
Let her too get home safe, your prayer,
not like that poor woman last night
dragged down Glovers Alley, raped there,
battered to a pulp. Still unnamed.
Your key in the door, you've made it back,
a chorus of birds predicting light.

3 *Man Sleeping*

How deep are you, how far under?
Here's rosemary I stole on my walk
and the first lilac from the Square
I lay them on the quilt. You talk
in your dreaming. *I am the beating tide,*
mine is the shore. Taste of the sea,
pulse of my heart. *Don't leave me,*
don't leave me. I dive beneath
and you stiffen to my mouth.
You'll be deep within me when you wake,
your pulse my own. Wave that I ride,
I'll take everything before you break.

4 *Full Moon*

She's up there. You'd know the pull,
stretching you tight as a drumhead,
anywhere. This morning lull
between the alarm and quitting the bed
you consider the scrawb on his back –
sigil of grief: the thumbscrew, the rack.
A paleskin staked on the desert floor
bound at ankle, at neck, at wrist,
no cavalry in sight to even the score.
This is the knife in the gut; this is its twist.

She's up there. Tonight they'll dish out
more downers in prison, in the mental
asylum, tonight there'll be more blood spilt
on the street, and you will howl
to her through the tattered cloud scrawled
across the windowpane, a howl fated
by the blemish on his shoulderblade.
Ask yourself: *To what shapechanger has he mated?*

5 *On the Warpath*

The full moon is drawing you tight
as a drumhead. Your face in the mirror
is cloudy, overcast. No sunny spells;
frost inland tonight.

Reconnoitre the terrain of the heart,
scan for high ground. Ambush, skirmish,
reprisal, this deadly game you play.
Give as good as you get.

Choose protective colouring, camouflage,
know your foe, every move of him,
every bar of his battle hymn.
Though the outward face is dead cas-

ual, within the self is coiled:
unsprung, the human, suddenly, wild.

Not Your Muse

I'm not your muse, not that creature
in the painting, with the beautiful body,
Venus on the half-shell. Can
you not see I'm an ordinary woman
tied to the moon's phases, bloody
six days in twenty-eight? Sure

I'd like to leave you in love's blindness,
cherish the comfort of your art, the way
it makes me whole and shining,
smooths the kinks of my habitual distress,
never mentions how I stumble into the day,
fucked up, penniless, on the verge of whining

at my lot. You'd have got away with it
once. In my twenties I often traded a bit
of sex for immortality. That's a joke.
Another line I swallowed, hook
and sinker. Look at you –
rapt, besotted. Not a gesture that's true

on that canvas, not a droopy breast,
wrinkle or stretchmark in sight.
But if it keeps you happy who am I
to charge in battledressed to force you test
your painted doll against the harsh light
I live by, against a brutal merciless sky.

Laburnum

You walk into an ordinary room
an ordinary evening, say
mid May, when the laburnum

hangs over the railings of the Square
and the city is lulled by eight o'clock
the traffic sparse, the air fresher.

You expect to find someone
waiting though now you live
alone. You've answered none

of your calls. The letters pile
up in the corner. The idea
persists that someone waits while

you turn the brass handle and knock
on the light. Gradually
the dark seeps into the room. You lock

out the night, scan a few books.
It's days since you ate.
The plants are dying – even the cactus,

shrivelled like an old scrotum
has given up the ghost. There's
a heel of wine in a magnum

you bought, when? The day
before? The day before that?
It's the only way

out. The cold sweats
begin. You knock back a few.
You've no clean clothes left.

He is gone. Say it.
Say it to yourself, to the room.
Say it loud enough to believe it.

You will live breath
by breath. The beat of your own heart
will scourge you. You'll wait

in vain, for he's gone from you.
And every night is a long
slide to the dawn you

wake to, terrified in your ordinary room
on an ordinary morning, say
mid May, say the time of laburnum.

Pillow Talk

These hot midsummer nights I whisper
assignations, trysts, heather beds
I'd like to lay you down in, remote beaches
we could escape to, watch
bonfire sparks mix with stars.
I want you to stay alive till we two
meet again, to hold the line, to ignore
the gossip traded about me in the marketplace.
I fall back on cliché, the small
change of an adulterous summer,
plots of half-hatched movies, theories
of forked lightning, how you make
the soles of my feet burn when I come.

What you don't hear is the other voice
when she speaks through me
beyond human pity or mercy. She wants you.
Put her eye on you the first time
she saw you. And I'm powerless,
a slave to her whim. She shall
have you. What can I do
when she speaks of white river stones,
elfin grots, her sacred birds?
I know she once tore a man apart,
limb from limb with her bare hands
in some rite in her bloody past.
My stomach turns at the hot
relentless stench of her history.

Nights you stare out
panic-stricken through the mask,
I think you may have heard her speak:
you realise that you ride a demon,
that the dark has no end to it.
Though I mean you no grief,
I cannot vouchsafe her intent. I fear
not all my healing arts can salve
the wound she has in store for you.

Silk

You dance in a length of shiny silk
lately acquired in a Tashkent bazaar,
charming me with every slink
of your hips, teeth aflash.

Haven't we met somewhere
before – by a gypsy fire
or in a blue domed marketplace
where slaves are traded for new gold?

If you seek to bind me
this summer with sex and cool melon,
don't bother. I'm already bound
and lost and falling fast,

tumbling head over heels
down the abyss.
                    To think
I've waited centuries for this!
You dancing in shiny silk

in the afternoon, stealing an hour
from work. And where
does it end?
                    Work and love:
the heart's hunger, the daily bread.

Breagaim Breagaim Breagaim
I woo I lie I woo
and if you walk away from me
on a hot city street

I'll not look after you,
                         but turn
into my own mystery. Though
it may take centuries to find you again,
dancing wantonly in silk.

'Would you jump into my grave as quick?'

Would you jump into my grave as quick?
my granny would ask when one of us took
her chair by the fire. You, woman,
done up to the nines, red lips a come on,
your breath reeking of drink
and your black eye on my man tonight
in a Dublin bar, think
first of the steep drop, the six dark feet.

The Ghost of My Mother Comforts Me

(after Van Morrison)

Do not fear, daughter,
when they lift their sticks, their stones,
when they hiss beneath their breaths –

Fallen woman, adulteress, breaker of marriage vows
made before a holy priest to an honourable man.

For you, daughter, there is no blame,
for you no portion of guilt,
for you're made in my likeness.
You can take the crucifixion from your voice.
I will stroke your forehead till you sleep,
till you pass over into the dreamworld
where we can walk together in gardens wet with rain
or fly along old star roads
or sit quietly near running water.

And when you wake refreshed
you'll be ready for their sticks, their stones,
their names that cannot hurt you.
Balance your gypsy soul, lodged
in the body given you, my daughter,
for your pleasure and as a tool for struggle,
against the weight of the world's troubles.
Take comfort in the knowledge that you are not alone.
There are many like you on the earth,
and you will be numbered among the warriors
when the great book is written.

Because I am your mother I will protect you
as I promised you in childhood.
You will walk freely on the planet,
my beloved daughter. Fear not
the lightning bolts of a Catholic god, or any other,
for I have placed my body and my soul between you and all harm.

Autobiography

She stalks me through the yellow flags.
If I look over my shoulder I will catch her
striding proud, a spear in her hand.
I have such a desperate need of her –
though her courage springs
from innocence or ignorance. I could lie with her
in the shade of the poplars, curled
to a foetal dream on her lap, suck
from her milk of fire to enable me fly.
Her face is my own face unblemished;
her eyes seapools, reflecting lichen,
thundercloud; her pelt like watered silk
is golden. She guides me to healing herbs
at meadow edges. She does not speak
in any tongue I recognise.
She is mother to me, young
enough to be my daughter.

The other one waits in gloomy hedges.
She pounces at night. She knows I've no choice.
She says: 'I am your future.
Look on my neck, like a chicken's
too old for the pot; my skin moults
in papery flakes. Hear it rustle?
My eyes are the gaping wounds
of newly opened graves. Don't turn
your nose up at me, madam.
You may have need of me yet.
I am your ticket underground.' And yes
she has been suckled at my own breast.
I breathed deep of the stench of her self –
the stink of railway station urinals,
of closing-time vomit, of soup lines
and charity shops. She speaks
in a human voice and I understand.
I am mother to her, young
enough to be her daughter.

I stand in a hayfield – midday, midsummer,
my birthday. From one breast
flows the Milky Way, the starry path,
a sluggish trickle of pus from the other.
When I fly off I'll glance back
once, to see my husk sink into the grasses.
Cranesbill and loosestrife will shed
seeds over it like a blessing.

'Not alone the rue in my herb garden...'

Not alone the rue in my herb garden
passes judgement, but the eight foot
high white foxgloves among the greys
of wormwood, santolina, lavender,
the crimson rose at our cottage door,
the peas holding for dear life to their sticks
and the smaller drowning salad stuff.
The weeds grow lush and lovely
at midsummer, honeysuckle roving
through the hawthorn: my garden
at Eslin ferociously passing judgement.

We built this soil together, husband;
barrow after barrow load of peat
sieved through an old chip strainer
and the heaps of rotted manure
pushed over frosty paths on still
midwinter days, or when an east wind
chewed at our knuckles. Cranky
of a morning when the range acted up,
we still saved wood ash and dug it in,
by Christmas laid a mulch of hay
and tucked it all up safe in beds,
turned off the light and spent the most
of January and February, the bitterest days,
at chess, or poem and story making.

You were beautiful in my father's
ravelled jumper, staring at the rain,
or painting revelations of the hag
that scared the living daylights out of me.
One canvas was blacker than
the lower pits of hell after an eternity
when even the scourging fire has gone out
and the tortured souls are silenced.

O heart of my husband, I thought,
how little have I fathomed thee,
when you went and overpainted it
on a St Brigid's Day of snow and crocuses,
with a green-eyed young fiddler,
named it *Mystery Dame with Red Hair*.

We built this garden together, husband;
germinated seeds in early spring,
gambling with a crystal dice,
moon calendars and almanacs,
risked seedlings to a late black frost,
wept at loss – but some survived
to thrive a summer of aching backs.
A festive air when the poles went up
and scarlet runners coiled along the twine.
Mornings I walked out after a shower

had tamped the dust and turned
the volume way up on birdsong,
on scent, on colour, I counted myself
the luckiest woman born, to gain such
an inland kingdom, three wild
rushy acres, edged by the Eslin
trickily looping us below the hill,
our bass line to the Shannon
and the fatal rhythm of the Atlantic swell.

I did not cast it off lightly,
the yoke of work, the years of healing,
of burying my troubled dead
with every seed committed to the earth,
judging their singular, particular needs,
nurturing them with sweat and prayer
to let the ghosts go finally from me
with every basket of the harvest
I garnered in golden light for our table,
something singing in me all the while,
a song of fate, of fortune, of a journey,
a twisty road that led away from you,
my husband of the sea-scarred eyes.

Now that I return to visit you,
abandoned gardens, abandoned husband,
abandoned cat and dog and chickens,
abandoned quilts and embroideries,
high piled books, my dusty drafts,
a life I stitched together out of love,
and we sit together by the window
in the summer light, the sculptural
clouds of June, their whimsical shadows
oblivious of the grief on our faces,
in sorrow at what we built and lost
and never will rebuild, O my friend,
do not turn on me in hatred,
do not curse the day we met.

Berlin Diary, 1991

1 *At the Pergamon*

The swastika at the centre
of the terracotta plate
behind security glass
in the Pergamon Museum
looks so wholly innocent.
I try to imagine the day of the potter,
a Sumerian day in 230 BC
by the bank of the Euphrates perhaps,
the clay centring on the wheel,
the thumb brought to bear
still there in the fine ridging
at the rim. This plate –
balance of held and holding,
the cold air of the museum,
the hum of the air conditioning,
the drone of a tour guide,
and the boots, the boots, the boots
of the guard echoing. My head
begins to spin.
         The plate
begins to spin. Swastika!
Black spinning sun of my own black pupil
thrown back from the glass. My eye
and swastika one
            black spinning sun!

I did not plan it but the clothes I chose that morning for the damp
day that's in it – long navy overcoat, grey silk headscarf, and in
my left ear a blue stone – make me look like a Turkish woman.

And I am bound for the Turkish market at Kreuzberg. On the
U-Bahn and the S-Bahn and the trams, so many graffiti swastikas
my eyes are aching. I break my journey at Rosa Luxembourg Platz
because I like the name.

A man up a ladder is postering over a street sign: Carrot Street.
Carrot Street? I ask why. *All names Communist gone with the Wall.*
There will be Cabbage Street and Turnip Street and Rutabaga
Street and Gherkin Street.

I have no gift to bring home to my friend, and the mist is
thickening and night coming on. I come to a U-Bahn. I ask direc-
tions to Kreuzberg. The man behind the counter nearly spits in my
face. Misdirects me. I've a three mile walk along the canal: the
lindens, the odd citizen walking a dog, a gang of mean looking
youths, all looming out of the mist.

I am considering the nature of betrayal and the circumstances in
an Izmir bazaar, his eye suddenly caught by the blue luminescence
of the stone that now adorns my left ear. *The sign of one who's
chosen the path of the warrior rather than the path of the lover*, he
said when he gave it to me.

I'm trying to work all this out in iambic, trying to find the strong
steady pulse of my walkabout in words. But there's too much
danger at the edges, and I need all my concentration for reading
the street. Visibility is down to a few yards and I've no way of
knowing what will come at me next out of the mist. Another gang
could materialise; or the same gang from twenty minutes ago could
be coming back to get me having only now processed the signals
of my garb.

When my friend gave me the earring he said it reminded him
of the Miraculous Medal his mother used pin on his gansy when
he was a boy, and followed it with a long rigmarole on Mariology,
Earth goddesses, the power of the female, mid-Eastern moon wor-
ship, blue as a healing colour, as Mary's colour. When I finally find
the market they are packing up their wares. I choose a jet and gold
anklet. I pay the jewel hawker the marks I owe her and she wraps
it up. A blue stone glitters at her throat, another on her baby's
blanket. *Good luck*, she says, *and health to wear it.*

3 *Handmade*

Your manifesto on my body
the yellow bruise on my breast
the exact same colour as the willow
at my window on Majakowskiring.

The morning I left Dublin you were telling me a story –
a suppressed genesis. How Lilith
who pre-dated Eve went about the garden
and asked each creature, each plant,
to tell her its original name.
I pictured her stooped to a mandrake. *Mandragora Officianarum.*
What the plant said to her,
or she to it for that matter, is a mystery.

We call things by their given names
as I imagine Adam meant for us to do
strutting round the garden –
You Giraffe! Me God'sman! and poor
spare-ribbed Eve tempted
by the snake totem of her wiser sister
gets them shagged into the wilderness.

A young man falls in love with Truth and searches the wide world for her. He finds her in a small house, in a clearing, in a forest. She is old and stooped. He swears himself to her service – to chop wood, to carry water, to collect the root, the stem, the leaf, the flowering top, the seed of each plant she needs for her work.

Years go by. One day the young man wakes up longing for a child. He goes to the old woman and asks to be released from his oath so that he may return to the world. *Certainly*, she says, *but on one condition: you must tell them that I am young and that I am beautiful.*

Smokestack, shunting train,
cobbles scored where
her high heels have graven
ghost music in the mist.
I'm searching for my mother
after another war.

She was broody, like Sophie,
a golden hen in a story she'd tell me
to keep the nightmares away.

Ghost music on Stargartenstrasse
her high heels fragmenting cobbles,
my golden broody hen.

Oak leaves trodden to dust,
the army marches past
smokestack, shunting train.
We'll not pass this way again.

I remember this episode. A German friend, a native of Berlin, has come to visit me on Papa Stour, a small island in the Shetland Islands. The first time he needs a shit, I give him a shovel and tell him to walk to the wild side of the island. From then on he calls the place *The Shitlands*. Close to the end of his stay we are sitting by the range after a long day gathering fuel. It's been hard work; mostly retrieving pine poles from a deep cove – no path down, straight over the cliff on a rope – but a good haul to be traded for coal or burnt itself. A fortnight's heat, a fortnight's writing and hot water worth of pine. It's two in the morning. There's the dusky light of this far northern midsummer, the *simmer dim* as the people around call it. He's picking out a tune on my Epiphone, humming. It's a Dylan song – *when you got nothing, you got nothing to lose.* I'm working through a basket of mending. I'm pleased with a patch on my jeans, the tricky way I have found to set it in, following the contours of my own ass. Neat. I embroider a small *Om* in white silk for luck on the crotch, though any man now would reach a *vagina dentata* rather than *The Gates of Awe*. He asks me to mend his waistcoat, *a tear, a couple of stitches would do it, it was my grandfather's.* I estimate. Two hours work. A darning job on the heavy worsted; and a finicky delicate stitching needed for the lining. Silk? A button gone. Have I a match? What's this? In the candlelight I make out the raised pattern on the remaining buttons. *Swastikas? Was your grandfather a Nazi?* Blurted out into what becomes a moment's terror – a look of pure hatred. I cannot unpick those words.

I fix the waistcoat carefully. You would have to look hard to find the mending. I strengthen some seams and sponge away the shiny grime at the neck, drape it above the range. If I hold anything of that day forever it will be his face staring down at me over the cliff's edge as he feeds out the rope with great care and concentration, my life in his hands.

The Wounded Child

1

First – gird yourself. Put on
a talisman. It may be precious
metal or common stone.

What matters is you believe
it powerful, ensurer of
a protective zone to ward off evil,

what matters is *baraka*
from years of kindly use; or that it be
a token of a good time, like a

night under a lucky star,
untroubled, with a gentle man
who means you no harm,

or a ring given in friendship –
a calm room, maybe spring,
the light spinning out, you sip

tea and talk long into darkness
of old lives and dreamtimes,
journeys that brought you near bliss.

2

Whatever you wear you'll be strange.
This is battledress. Paint your face,
put feathers in your hair, arrange
your skirts, your skins, your lace.

Your own eyes stare out clear,
unfazed, from the bedroom mirror.
Though the mask is not familiar
your own eyes stare out. With no fear.

You are able for this.

3

Somewhere in the girl you once were
is the wounded child. Find her.
You have to find her.

She is lonely. Terrified. Curled
to a foetal grip in a tight place,
sobbing her heart out. The world

is a man with big hands
and sharp teeth. The world
is a ton of bricks, sand

in her mouth, a huge weight
on her chest. She has no breath
to speak of it. Her fate

is unwritten, silent, mute.
Remember her? Remember
her splitting apart. Tell her truth.

4

Pick her up. *Go on!*
Hold her close to you.
Hold her to your breast.
If you cannot find the words
at first, hum the tune.
They will come eventually;
like a spell or a prayer
they are already there.

When she has quietened
tell her the story of the Russian doll:

A child, lost in a forest, curls in the lip of a fallen birch among
fern and moss. She sleeps. Dreams of her mother. She clutches a
wooden doll. The woodcutter draws near. She hears beat of axe,
saw's clean song. Freed of bole, of branches, the stump swings back,
closes over her like a great mouth. And still she dreams, opening
doll after doll, seeking the kernel carved from birch heartwood,
seeking the smallest doll she can hold in her palm. Fire consumes
the forest; smoke obscures the sun. Deer and wolf alike flee the
hungry tongues. A birch seedling thrives on the spot, thrives
through the seasons until it is the finest sapling in the forest. The
girl pushes through rings, sheds silver bark on the snow. The yel-
low years fall, ripple out forever. Passing, you might hear her
voice and name it *Wind-in-Leaves*. Your heart would ache with
loneliness. She dreams of nut within shell, scrolls back to birth of
glacier, forward to death of sun. The woodcutter finds her pliant
to the whim of the wind. She surrenders to beat of axe, to saw's
clean song, welcomes the familiar refrain.

5

When your story is told
give her the Russian doll.
Make her peel away layer after layer
till she gains the inmost figure
from the birch's heartwood whittled
so small the face has lost its human guise.
Say: *Take this in your first, love,*
grip tight and feel
glacier grind mountain to dust,
fire gallop across the taiga,
sunlight pulse through your leaves,
snow melt to nourish your roots;
bend with grace before the wind's might,
embrace beat of axe, saw's clean song.

Rescue the child
                from her dark spell!
Rescue the child
                from her dark spell!
Rescue the child.

25 February 1992

Island Burial

They bury their dead as quick as they can
before the shapechanging shames them
and gets them branded as witches.
I know a family had to watch their dead daughter
turn into a hare before their eyes.
They coffined her quick but swear
they heard paws against the coffin lid
as they lowered her down, as the clay fell.

1 *Song of the Grave*

I am the grave waiting
patient receptive damp
for my hare girl in flux

when she's entered her hare self
I'll close like a fist
an end to her thumping rut

a long time hence
when you prise open my fingers
her bones on my palm

know I have cherished her

2 *Prayer at the Graveside*

Burying our dead
Flesh to dust
Dust on the wind
Ash on your brow
Song of the yew
Chalice of darkness

hare field witch
burning hare crack
cloud sea rock
a bye long sleep

hare lope green
path gate stream
sun white stone
belly breath come

hare heron cry
sand grain star
foot before foot
up stony road

hare paws hare
paws beat on wood
hare spent kick
blue eye watch

knife rope cut
home safe feather

Dream Filter

Before you were born,
I made a dream filter
to ensure you clear dreamings

for the whole of your childhood,
to the exact specifications
of a tribe I read about

in *National Geographic*. First
I'd to clear my own dreams
and pass all my bad visions

into stones; then go on foot
to pure swift running water
near where it entered the sea

and cast each weighted stone
to the pebbly bed
where they could be washed to a calm

stonedness again. Only
then was I fit to begin.

                *

The finding of coppiced hazel,
the twisting of hempen twine,
the building of the dream filter

itself, took a full seven months.
Wait for a bird
to gift you some feathers.

On the walk to the hospital
down by the South Docks,
after a night spent in labour,

three slate-grey feathers there in my path.
I looked up and saw
a peregrine falcon hung in the air –

one of a pair that were nesting
on top of the gasometer.

*

This contraption
made of hazel and hemp
and a few tail feathers

is fixed tonight above your cradle.
One day you'll ask
what it's all about.

And what can I tell you?
What can I possibly say?

Blessing
(for Tony Curtis)

Not to the colony for artists
not to the walled university
but to the demented asylum
I'll go when the moon is up
in the day sky, I'll go

and snatch a song from a stranger's mouth.

They have been speaking so long
in riddles they teach you
the heart for a child breaking,
the heart breaking for a child
is nothing more than a shift
of light on a slate roof
after rain, and the elderberry's
purpling shade is as much
as you'll know of grieving.

They have been speaking so long
in riddles the world believes at last
in enigma, the earth understands
in her beguiling work –
    leaf, stone, wave.

To the demented asylum I'll go
for succour from a stranger's mouth:
    leaf crown you
        wave repeat you
            stone secure your grave

Home

I am the blind woman finding her way home by a map of tune.
When the song that is in me is the song I hear from the world
I'll be home. It's not written down and I don't remember the words.
I know when I hear it I'll have made it myself. I'll be home.

A version I heard once in Leitrim was close, a wet Tuesday night
in the Sean Relig bar. I had come for the session, I stayed
for the vision and lore. The landlord called time,
the music dried up, the grace notes were pitched to the dark.
When the jukebox blared out *I'd only four senses and he left me
      senseless,*
I'd no choice but to take to the road. On Grafton Street in November
I heard a mighty sound: a travelling man with a didgeridoo
blew me clear to Botany Bay. The tune too far back to live in
but scribed on my bones. In a past life I may have been Kangaroo,
rocked in my dreamtime, convict ships coming o'er the foam.

In the Puzzle Factory one winter I was sure I was home.
The talking in tongues, the riddles, the rhymes, struck a chord
that cut through the pharmaceutical haze. My rhythm catatonic,
I lulled myself back to the womb, my mother's heart
beating the drum of herself and her world. I was tricked
by her undersong, just close enough to my own. I took then
to dancing; I spun like a Dervish. I swear I heard the subtle
music of the spheres. It's no place to live, but –
out there in space, on your own, hung aloft the night.
The tune was in truth a mechanical drone;
I was a pitiful monkey jigging on cue. I came back to earth
with a land, to rain on my face, to sun in my hair. And grateful too.

The wisewomen say you must live in your skin, call *it* home,
no matter how battered or broken, misused by the world, you can
      heal.
This morning a letter arrived on the nine o'clock post.
The Department of Historical Reparation, and who did I blame?
The Nuns? Your Mother? The State? *Tick box provided,*
we'll consider your case. I'm burning my soapbox, I'm taking
the very next train. A citizen of nowhere, nothing to my name.

I'm on my last journey. Though my lines are all wonky
they spell me a map that makes sense. Where the song that is in me
is the song I hear from the world, I'll set down my burdens
and sleep. The spot that I lie on at last the place I'll call home.

Seed

The first warm day of spring
and I step out into the garden from the gloom
of a house where hope had died
to tally the storm damage, to seek what may
have survived. And finding some forgotten
lupins I'd sown from seed last autumn
holding in their fingers a raindrop each
like a peace offering, or a promise,
I am suddenly grateful and would
offer a prayer if I believed in God.
But not believing, I bless the power of seed,
its casual, useful persistence,
and bless the power of sun,
its conspiracy with the underground,
and thank my stars the winter's ended.